Environmental Science 1A03
Climate and Water
Lab Manual

Dr. Luc Bernier

January 2015

Contents

Part I: Organizational Information

Course Outline 7

Lecture and Lab Outline 15

Student Responsibility Contract 16

Faculty of Science Statement of Academic Dishonesty.......................................19

Interpretation of the Statement of Academic Dishonesty 21

Part II: Lab Test Preparation

Lab Test 1: Solar Geometry and Radiation Budgets 25

Lab Test 2: Environmental and Adiabatic Lapse Rates 31

Lab Test 3: Water Balance 35

Lab Test 4: Weather Maps 43

Part III: References and Acknowledgements 50

I. Organizational Information

Environmental Science 1A03
Climate and Water
Course Outline
January 2015

Instructor
Luc Bernier
GSB-202
Email: berniejm@mcmaster.ca

Instructional Assistant
Lisa Leoni
BSB 317D
Email: leonil@mcmaster.ca

Introduction

The primary aim of this course is to introduce students to the processes involved in weather, climate and the hydrologic cycle with an emphasis on human impacts on these processes. The course begins by examining the structure of Earth's atmosphere and global radiation budget. This will be followed by a discussion of atmospheric heating and cooling. Knowledge that the students gain from this section will be used to examine atmospheric stability, cloud development and precipitation. Students will use their understanding of the hydrologic cycle and of water balance to describe global climate patterns. Attention is given to both surface, atmospheric and soil water. Students will then consider how air moves in the atmosphere both on a local and global scale. The final section of the course examines anthropogenic impacts including air pollution, and the increase of the greenhouse effect. The course balances a large knowledge component with the development of personal transferable skills.

In this course students will be provided the opportunity to analyse data provided to them. Labs 1, 2, 3, and 4 will provide students an opportunity to develop their data manipulation, data interpretation and numerical skills. The final lab exercise involves students using weather maps, examining this data, and enhancing their analytical skills. The course includes frequent evaluations of lecture material through a series of online quizzes. The existence of these frequent evaluations will encourage students to further develop their time management skills.

Textbooks

1. Ahrens, C.D., Jackson, P.L., and Jackson, C.E.J., 2012. Meteorology Today. First Canadian Edition. Nelson Education Ltd, Toronto, Ontario, 616pp. ISBN-13: 978-0176500399.
2. Custom Courseware for ENVIR SCI 1A03.
3. Custom Courseware, Handbook for the Earth & Environmental Sciences Student (Available on Avenue to Learn).

Lectures

Lectures will occur on Tuesdays, and Wednesdays from 9:30am – 10:20am in MDCL-1305 as per the attached schedule. The Friday lecture period will not be used, unless announced otherwise during the term. ALL students are expected to attend ALL lectures. **Partial** lecture notes will be available on A2L. **It is the responsibility of the student to ensure that notes are obtained for any classes missed.**

The live lectures will be supplemented by Podcasts that will be posted on Avenue to Learn (A2L). **The material covered in these podcasts is just as important to your understanding of the course as the material covered during the live lectures.**

Students are NOT authorized to record the live lectures (video recording, audio recording; taking pictures, etc.) without explicit and documented approval from the course instructor. If approval is given, students are forbidden to redistribute this material through any platform (social media, etc.).

Evaluation Scheme

This course will consist of online quizzes, lab tests and a final exam. There will be 5 quizzes in the course covering lecture and textbook material. Quizzes are valued at 5% each and the lowest quiz mark will be dropped. Quizzes will be available on A2L (Avenue to Learn) for a 7-day period. Their schedule will be posted on A2L. It is the responsibility of the student to be aware of quiz start and end dates, and of dates for the lab tests. Please see the section titled *'Missed Work or Late Work'* for information regarding missed quizzes.

This course will also contain a Final Exam. The final exam will cover all lecture and textbook readings, as well as subjects covered by the lab tests. The final exam will consist of calculations, short and/or long answer questions.

Lab Tests (4 @ 7.5%)	30%
A2L quizzes (best 4 of 5 @ 5% each)	20%
i-Clicker Participation	10%
Final Exam	40%

Labs

You have been assigned a lab time by the registrar's office. Attendance at labs is mandatory. The first lab begins the week of January 19th. A complete lab schedule is attached.

The course will contain four lab tests. The topics are as follows:
Lab Test 1: Solar Geometry and Radiation Budgets
Lab Test 2: Environmental and Adiabatic Lapse Rates
Lab Test 3: Water Balance
Lab Test 4: Weather Maps

The introduction and background information for each Lab Test will be given during your assigned lab period. Each introduction will be accompanied by an online tutorial (podcast) released on Avenue to Learn (see attached schedule). **It is your responsibility to watch and listen to these tutorials, and to come prepared to lab.** The Lab Tests will also take place during the lab period, in the week following the lab test introduction. Please see the attached schedule for the dates of the lab introductions and lab tests.

ALL submitted tests MUST contain the following information: name, student ID number, course name and number (i.e. Envir Sc 1A03), test number (e.g. Lab Test 1), name of your teaching assistant (T.A), lab section number or day/ time of your lab section, and date. Tests submitted without this information will be penalized, i.e. 10% of the mark obtained will be deducted.

Active Participation during Lectures using i-Clicker

We will be using the i-Clicker during lectures. Clicker questions are part of every lecture, so bring your clicker to class every day. **If you have registered your i-Clicker and you click a response to at least 80% of clicker polls during the term, you will receive the full 10% clicker grade.**

If you respond to less than 80% of possible polls, your clicker grade is pro-rated, in the following manner:

% of polls participated to	Participation Mark %
80 or more	10 (full %)
75 to 79	9
70 to 74	8
60 to 69	7
50 to 59	6
40 to 49	5
30 to 39	4
20 to 29	3
10 to 19	2
1 to 9	1

The percentage of the polls you will have provided an answer to, and your i-Clicker Participation mark (out of 10) will be will be updated weekly on Avenue to Learn. To register your i-Clicker, please use your MacID here:

http://www1.iclicker.com/register-clicker/

No accommodations will be made for i-Clicker issues such as: lost devices, devices forgotten at home, dead batteries, mistakes in programming the Base Frequency, or malfunctioning devices. It is the student's responsibility to make sure that they have their i-Clicker with them for lecture, that the device is functioning properly, and that they know how to use it. Should

9

there be a discrepancy between the record of participation obtained from the i-Clicker Base System and a student's own personal tracking of her/his participation during the term, the record from the Base System will prevail.

Participation for marks will start to be recorded on Tuesday January 20th, 2015

Attendance and Emails Policy

Appointments can be scheduled with the instructor to help clarify the content of lectures. It is not the instructor's responsibility to go over an entire lecture with you, if you missed it. It is your responsibility to acquire the necessary information from classmates.

It is not appropriate to use email to ask detailed questions (including asking about what was discussed in lecture). As a general rule, you should not expect to receive answers to emails on weekends or late in the evening. Rather, emails will typically be responded to during regular working hours on weekdays, and as schedule allows. Emails sent 24 hours prior to, or on the test date will not be answered.

As a courtesy, and to ensure your emails are properly answered, you must include your name and student ID number in the email signature, and the course code and number (ENVIR SC 1A03). Emails must be sent from McMaster email accounts or they will not be read or responded to. **Emails sent from Avenue or within Avenue will not be responded to**. Emails should be written in a professional manner, spell-checked and proof-read before sending them. The subject line **must** state for which course the query is about. Online discussion terminology (e.g. Twitter) must be avoided.

Course Contract

All students are required to read and understand the Student Responsibility Contract included in this outline (a copy can also be found in your courseware). This contract is a component of the course outline, and extends as well as specifies a number of course policies students must be aware of. Academic Integrity is an important issue at McMaster University and it is the responsibility of all students to understand what constitutes Academic Dishonesty. All students must agree to the Course Policies and demonstrate an understanding of what constitutes Academic Dishonesty by completing the Academic Integrity and Responsibility (AIR) Quiz. **All students are required to complete the AIR Quiz on Avenue and score a grade of greater or equal to 90% by <u>Friday, January 30th, 2015 at 4:30pm</u>. Students will receive a 25% deduction on Lab Test 1 if the AIR Quiz has not been completed successfully by the deadline.**

Avenue to Learn (A2L) Information

URL: http://avenue.mcmaster.ca/

A2L is an online system which will be used in this class for communicating information relating to the course (e.g. lecture notes, lab preparation etc.). To log in to A2L use your MUGSI login and password. See the A2L home page above for more instructions if you need them. **It is the student's responsibility to check A2L regularly (i.e. AT LEAST twice a week) for updates.**

Students should be aware that, when they access the electronic components of this course, private information such as first and last names, user names for the McMaster e-mail accounts, and program affiliation may become apparent to all other students in the same course. The available information is dependent on the technology used. Continuation in this course will be deemed consent to this disclosure. If you have any questions or concerns about such disclosure please discuss this with the course instructor.

If you encounter any technical problems with this service go to the following website for support: **http://avenue.mcmaster.ca/help/.**

Please note that it is not the responsibility of the teaching staff of ENVIR SC 1A03 to assist you with A2L issues.

Missed or Late work

If you miss a Lab Test for a legitimate reason you must follow the following 2 steps:

1) You can report absences that last up to 5 days using the McMaster Student Absence Form (MSAF). Please see the section titled *'McMaster Student Absence Form (MSAF)'* for further information. Do not bring a doctor's note to your instructor or T.A

2) You **must** contact your instructor to find out what accommodations, if any, will be made for a missed test. Your marks for a missed lab test may be applied to the final exam (e.g. the 7.5% for a missed lab test will be applied to the final exam making it worth 47.5% of your final mark).

If you do not complete these two steps within **5 days** of the missed evaluation you will receive a mark of zero.

NO accommodation will be made for extra-curricular activities (participation to varsity teams, academic clubs, etc.) without students having documentation approved by their Associate Dean's office **in advance**. Accommodations, **approved by the Associate Dean's office**, will need to be discussed **a minimum of two weeks** before a course component will be missed or due.

As online quizzes will be available for a 7-day period, MSAFs will NOT be accepted for missed quizzes; see the section titled *'McMaster Student Absence Form (MSAF)'*. Marks for a missed quiz, with appropriate supporting documentation, will count towards the lowest quiz mark for the course. Marks for additional missed quizzes will be allocated towards your final exam (e.g. the 5% for a missed quiz will be applied to the final exam making it worth 45% of your final mark).

MSAFs will NOT be accepted for missed participation; see the section titled *'McMaster Student Absence Form (MSAF)'* for absences of a longer duration. Accommodations for missed in-class participation (i-Clicker) will **only** be possible if the absence, supported by documentation, lasts **21 days or more without interruption**. Only in that instance will the percentage of the questions missed be applied to the final exam (e.g. if 50% of the Clicker questions asked during the term were missed, then half of the participation mark, 5%, will be applied to the final exam making it worth 45% of your final mark).

Students who miss a Lab Test without either submitting the MSAF or documentation approved by their Associate Dean's office will automatically receive a mark of zero (0) for that lab test.

McMaster Student Absence Form (MSAF)

If you are absent from the university for a minor medical reason, lasting fewer than 5 days, you may report your absence, once per term, without documentation, using the McMaster Student Absence Form. Absences for a longer duration or for other reasons must be reported to your Faculty/Program office, with documentation, and relief from term work may not necessarily be granted.

When using the MSAF, report your absence to **berniejm@mcmaster.ca**. You must then contact your instructor immediately (normally <u>within 2 working days</u>) by email at **berniejm@mcmaster.ca** to learn what relief may be granted for the work you have missed, and relevant details such as revised deadlines, or time and location of a make-up evaluation.

Please note that the MSAF may not be used for term work worth 30% or more, nor can it be used for the final examination.

Please note: students who use the MSAF, but who do not contact the instructor within the <u>2 working days</u> period, may not be granted any relief.

Reporting Quiz Issues

1) You have **one week** after a quiz has been completed and the results released, to report an issue. Please make sure to take a good look at your quiz results once they are released.

2) Issues that are reported via email to the course instructor will not be addressed. **<u>You need to complete the *Quiz Issue Reporting Form* on A2L for them to be dealt with</u>.** A reporting form will be available for each quiz.

3) You **must** answer the following questions in the reporting form:

- which specific attempt you want the course instructor to look into,
- which specific question number you want the course instructor to look into,
- the full text of the question,
- if relevant, which option is identified as the correct option,
- if relevant, which option you believe is the correct one, and why.
- and/or any other detail that you think is relevant: missing figure, repetition of the options, incomplete question, material covered by the question, etc.

4) Unless stated otherwise, the issue(s) reported will only be addressed once a quiz is over; not while it is still active. The issue(s) will then be dealt with as quickly as possible.

Mark Appeals and A2L grades

You will have one week from the date that marks for an evaluation (e.g. lab test) are released to appeal your mark. If you wish to appeal a mark, you must leave a written note (including your name, McMaster email address, and student ID number) in the ENVIR SC 1A03 drop box stating which evaluation you want to be investigated, and justifying why you wish to have the evaluation looked after. You must also attach to this note the material to be reviewed. If the written request is found to be insufficiently justified (e.g. simply wanting a higher mark is insufficient), the matter will not be further investigated.

Your marks will be recorded on A2L. It is your responsibility to check that all marks entered are recorded properly. You must notify the instructor about any errors with regards to how your marks are entered. You have until 48 hours prior to the final exam to report any A2L mark issues.

Academic Dishonesty

You are expected to exhibit honesty and use ethical behaviour in all aspects of the learning process. Academic credentials you earn are rooted in principles of honesty and academic integrity.

Academic dishonesty is to knowingly act or fail to act in a way that results or could result in unearned academic credit or advantage. This behaviour can result in serious consequences, e.g. the grade of zero on an assignment, loss of credit with a notation on the transcript (notation reads: "Grade of F assigned for academic dishonesty"), and/or suspension or expulsion from the university.

It is your responsibility to understand what constitutes academic dishonesty. For information on the various types of academic dishonesty please refer to the Academic Integrity Policy, located at
 http://www.mcmaster.ca/academicintegrity

The following illustrates only three forms of academic dishonesty:

1. Plagiarism, e.g. the submission of work that is not one's own or for which other credit has been obtained.
2. Improper collaboration in group work.
3. Copying or using unauthorized aids in tests and examinations.

Acknowledgement of Course Policies

Your registration and continuous participation (e.g. on A2L., in the classroom, etc.) to the various learning activities of ENVIR SC 1A03 will be considered to be an implicit acknowledgement of the course policies outlined above, included in the Student Course Contract, or of any other that may be announced during lecture and/or on A2L. **It is your responsibility to read this course outline, to familiarize yourself with the course policies and to act accordingly.**

Lack of awareness of the course policies cannot be invoked at any point during this course for failure to meet them. It is your responsibility to ask for clarification on any policies that you do not understand. The instructor reserves the right to modify elements of the course and will notify students accordingly (in class and post any changes to the course A2L.). **The lecture schedule is only a guideline and may be modified during the course of the class.**

The instructor and university reserve the right to modify elements of the course during the term. The university may change the dates and deadlines for any or all courses in extreme circumstances. If either type of modification becomes necessary, reasonable notice and communication with the students will be given with explanation and the opportunity to comment on changes. It is the responsibility of the student to check their McMaster email and course websites weekly during the term and to note any changes.

Lecture and Lab Schedule

Week Beginning	Weekday	Topic	Lab Introduction / Lab Test	Readings
Jan. 5	T W F	Introduction to the Course Weather, Climate and Earth's Atmosphere NO LECTURE		Chapter 1 Chapter 18
Jan. 12	T W F	Atmospheric Pressure and Density Global Energy Balance NO LECTURE		Chapter 1 Chapter 2
Jan. 19	T W F	Global Energy Balance - *continued* Variation of Surface Temperature NO LECTURE	Lab 1 Introduction – Solar Angle and Radiation Budgets	Chapter 2 Chapter 3
Jan. 26	T W F	Variation of Surface Temperature - *continued* Atmospheric Moisture NO LECTURE	*Lab Test 1* - Solar Angle and Radiation Budgets	Chapter 3 Chapter 4
Feb. 2	T W F	The Adiabatic Process Clouds NO LECTURE	Lab 2 Introduction – Environmental Lapse Rates	Chapter 6 Chapter 5
Feb. 9	T W F	Precipitation, Snow and Ice The Hydrologic Cycle and the Water Balance NO LECTURE	*Lab Test 2* – Environmental Lapse Rates	Chapter 7
Feb. 16	T W F	**READING WEEK**		
Feb. 23	T W F	Winds and Pressure Major Wind Systems NO LECTURE	NO LAB	Chapter 8 Chapter 9
Mar. 2	T W F	Atmospheric Circulation Oceanic Circulation NO LECTURE	Lab 3 Introduction – Water Balance	Chapter 10
Mar. 9	T W F	Air Masses and Fronts Midlatitude Systems and Storms NO LECTURE	*Lab Test 3* – Water Balance	Chapter 11 Chapter 12
Mar. 16	T W F	Thunderstorms and Tornadoes Hurricanes NO LECTURE	Lab 4 Introduction – Weather Maps	Chapter 14 Chapter 15
Mar. 23	T W F	Climate Variability and Feedbacks Climate Change and Human Interactions with Climate NO LECTURE	*Lab Test 4* – Weather Maps	Chapter 16
Mar. 30	T W F	Global Climate Climates of the World **GOOD FRIDAY - NO LECTURE**		Chapter 17
Apr. 6	T W	GIS and Environmental Science Final Exam Review		

This lecture schedule is only a guideline and may be modified during the course of the class.

ENVIR SC 1A03 - Student Responsibility Contract:

Being a university student requires you to assume a level of responsibility towards your academic career. Rules and Regulations regarding coursework change during the transition from high school to university as well as varying between Faculties and courses at McMaster. We want to ensure that you (the student) understand and acknowledge certain aspects of how this course operates.

All students are required to read and understand this course contract. This contract is a component of the course outline, and extends as well as specifies a number of course policies students must be aware of. **All students must agree to the course policies and demonstrate their understanding of Academic Integrity by completing the Academic Integrity and Responsibility (AIR) Quiz on Avenue. Students will receive a -25% deduction on Lab Test 1 if they have not successfully completed (grade of ≥ 90%) the AIR Quiz.**

Lab Tests:

I am aware that all submitted tests will need to include ALL of the following information: name, student ID number, course name and number (i.e. Envir Sc 1A03), test number (e.g. Lab Test 1), name of my TA, Lab section number or day/ time of my lab section, and date. I am aware that tests submitted without this information will be penalized, i.e. 10% of the mark I obtained will be subtracted.

☐ I understand and agree to the course policies with respect to Assignment Submission.

Illness:

If I am sick or have another extraordinary circumstance that results in my missing course-work (e.g. deadlines), it is my responsibility to get proper medical (or other) documentation. I understand that absences that last up to 5 days must be reported using the McMaster Student Absence Form (MSAF). I also understand that a maximum of 1 MSAFs may be filed per term and MSAFs cannot be filed during examination periods. If I am absent for more than 5 days or exceed the maximum of 1 request per term I must visit my Associate Dean's Office. It is my responsibility, after submitting this documentation, to contact the Instructor to discuss what, if any, accommodations will be made with respect to any missed work. **I have <u>one week</u> from the date of a lab test to complete this process; otherwise I will receive a mark of zero.**

I have <u>2 days</u> once a MSAF has been submitted to contact the Instructor, otherwise I will receive a mark of zero.

Furthermore, I am not to assume that I do not have to complete any missed work; it is up to my Instructor (not my T.A.) to determine what, if any, accommodations will be made. **I also understand that if I miss a lab test without approved documentation I will automatically receive a mark of zero (0) for that lab test.**

☐ I understand and agree to the course policies with respect to Illness.

Mark Appeals and A2L Grades:

I have one week from the date that a lab test (or online quiz) is returned to class (or once results are released) to appeal my mark. If I wish to appeal a grade, I must submit to my T.A. a written note justifying why I wish to have the component remarked, with the test attached. If my T.A. considers the written justification to be insufficient (e.g. simply wanting a higher grade is insufficient), the assignment will not be re-graded. If the justification is considered sufficient, the entire test will get re-graded. I therefore understand that my mark can increase or decrease.

My marks will be recorded on A2L. It is my responsibility to check that all grades entered into A2L are recorded properly. I must notify my T.A. about any errors with regards to how my mark was entered. I have until 48 hours prior to the final exam to discuss any A2L mark issues.

☐ I understand and agree to the course policies with respect to Appeals and Avenue Grades.

Academic Integrity:

Academic Integrity is a very important issue at McMaster University. It is my responsibility to understand what constitutes Academic Dishonesty, and to complete the A2L module Academic Integrity and Responsibility. Among possible forms of academic dishonesty are: cheating on tests or exams by using unauthorized aids; inappropriately collaborating in group work; and plagiarism. This extends to A2L as well, and sharing of answers on the Discussion board constitutes a form of academic dishonesty as well. For more information on what constitutes Academic Dishonesty, I should consult the University policy, and its interpretation by the Faculty of Science as included in the Custom Courseware of the course.

Furthermore, and of particular importance for this course I am aware that I must source ALL information that is not my own. If I submit an assignment with inadequate referencing I may face serious academic consequences (e.g. mark deductions, grade of zero, notation on my transcript, etc.).

☐ I understand and agree to the course policies with respect to Academic Integrity.

Lab Attendance/T.A. Emails:

Labs are held to enhance the lectures, as well as to provide essential information for my lab tests. I understand that lab attendance is mandatory in this course. I am aware that if I miss a lab I will receive a grade of zero on the lab unless a MSAF or approved documentation is provided to my Associate Dean's office and arrangements are made with the course Instructor.

It is not appropriate to use email to ask detailed questions (including asking about what was discussed in lab). T.A's are not expected to answer emails on weekends or late in the evening. Rather, emails will typically be responded to during regular working hours on weekdays, and as schedule allows. Emails on assignment due dates will not be answered.

As a courtesy, and to ensure that emails reach my T.A. or the instructor, I will use the following subject: line: ENVIR SC 1A03 - my name and student ID number. My name and student ID number should also be included in the email signature. Emails must be sent from McMaster email accounts or they will not be read or responded to. Emails should be written in a professional manner, spell-checked and proof-read before sending them. Online discussion terminology (e.g. Twitter) must be avoided.

☐ I understand and agree to the course policies with respect to Attendance & Email.

Student Conduct:

I acknowledge that my behaviour in all aspects of this course should meet the standards of the McMaster University Student Code of Conduct. I understand that any inappropriate behaviour directed against any of my colleagues, my T.A, or the instructor will not be tolerated. Disruptive behaviour during labs such as talking while a T.A. presents information, or constantly being late to lab, will also not be tolerated.

Students are encouraged to check the course discussion board on A2L on a regular basis and to ask questions in this forum rather than via email. If a question arises, in all likelihood many other students in the course will have it as well. This also means that the A2L Discussion Board is an extension of the classroom. These spaces are to be considered inclusive and safe. Abuse, ridicule, slander, inappropriate language, and discrimination towards the instructor, teaching staff, and other students will not be tolerated in any capacity.

☐ I understand and agree to the course policies with respect to Student Conduct.

Acknowledgement of Understanding of Course Policies:

☐ I have read the Student Responsibility Contract and acknowledge that I fully understand and will abide by these course policies. I understand that it is my responsibility to ask for clarification on any policies that I do not understand.

Faculty of Science
Statement of Academic Dishonesty

Introduction

The University Senate has approved a set of resolutions that define academic dishonesty and outline the procedure to be followed in the event that a student is charged with academic dishonesty. Most of the following information has been abstracted or summarized from the Senate Resolutions and further details can be obtained from the Office of the Secretary of the Senate or the Office of the Associate Dean.

Purpose of a University

The main purpose of a university is to encourage and facilitate the pursuit of knowledge and scholarship. The attainment of this purpose requires the individual integrity of all the scholars. Academic dishonesty, in whatever form, is ultimately destructive of the values of the University; it is furthermore unfair and discouraging to the majority of students who pursue their studies honestly. The University thus states unequivocally that it demands scholarly integrity from all members and that it will impose sanctions on those who directly or indirectly contribute to the weakening of this integrity.

Academic Dishonesty

Academic dishonesty is not qualitatively different from other types of dishonesty. It consists of misrepresentation in an attempt to deceive. In an academic setting this may take any number of forms such as : copying or the use of unauthorized aids in tests, examinations and laboratory reports; plagiarism; the submission of work that is not one's own or for which previous credit has been obtained, unless the previously submitted work has been presented as such to the instructor of the second course and has been deemed acceptable for credit by the instructor of that course; aiding and abetting another student's dishonesty; giving false information for the purpose of gaining admission, credits, etc.

Most of the above instances of dishonesty are clearly attempts to cheat or falsify. Plagiarism, however, may be less obvious than other instances of dishonesty, especially for the student new to the University. The following paragraph attempts to make clear the distinction between proper and improper use of source material in essays, assignments, lab reports, and other written work.

Direct quotation (i.e. use of another writer's exact words) is proper so long as the quotation is an exact copy, including punctuation, or the original. It must be enclosed in quotation marks and be fully documented as to source by a footnote or by a reference in parentheses directly following the quotation. When a passage is not exactly reproduced but is summarized or

19

paraphrased, it should not be enclosed in quotation marks but must nevertheless be similarly documented. Each such use of another's material, whether that material is published or unpublished, must have its own footnote or reference. It is not sufficiently simply to list the source in the reference given at the end of the assignment.

Tests and Examinations

In all tests and examinations, including take-home examinations, you are expected to work strictly on your own using only aids authorized for use in the examination or test area by invigilators. Use of other aids or assistance to other students during tests or examinations will be dealt with under the procedures outlined in the Senate Resolutions and can involve expulsion from the University. Examination regulations must be followed and any attempt to communicate with others about any matter is an infringement of these regulations.

Laboratory and Project Assignments

In some Faculties laboratory and project assignments are part of the learning process. In such activities it will be necessary to work in groups in which case it will be your responsibility to ensure that you make an effective contribution to the activity. The laboratory or project instructor will be able to clarify the amount of collaboration acceptable.

Interpretation of the Faculty of Science Statement on Academic Dishonesty

Introduction

In the last several years it has become apparent that a large number of students are unsure/unaware of exactly what is and what is not permitted with regards to plagiarism. The cause of this uncertainty is not the focus of this interpretation rather the intention is to identify the most frequently encountered pitfalls and to make students aware of the consequences of plagiarism.

Tests and Exams

Most students understand that tests must be worked on independently. The use of unauthorized aids (e.g. cheat sheets) or copying/discussing during the test period will result in a mark of zero on the test/exam. Senate Resolutions allow for the possible expulsion from the University of a student involved in cheating of this type.

Lab Exercises

This is the section of the course that the largest numbers of students are unaware/unsure of what constitutes plagiarism.

One of the most frequently asked questions is "may we work on this exercise together?". The answer is a resounding **YES**. Yes, you may discuss the question together, yes, you can locate relevant information from the text or library together **BUT** you must each hand in your own version of the lab answers. This means that the written answer must be in your own words and no two students could have identical written answers. It also means that each student must complete any graphing independently. All the graphs completed for this course may be computer generated. Information obtained from the text or other sources must be referenced using the author's date referencing system. The bibliographic information must then appear at the end of your lab in a section entitled References. For further details on reference style, refer to The Handbook for the Environmental Sciences Student in the School of Geography and Earth Sciences.

Part II: Lab Test Preparation

Lab Test 1 – Solar Geometry and Radiation Budgets

Preparation: Watch the Lab 1 Tutorial on A2L, complete the sample questions provided, and study/understand all equations and concepts

Worth: 7.5% of your final mark

Introduction: Week of January 19th

Lab Test 1: In Lab the week of January 26th

Solar Geometry

The Sun is the primary source of energy for most of the processes that operate at or near the Earth's surface. However, this energy is not available equally to all parts of the planet. It is important to understand the effects that Earth's simultaneous motions of axial rotation and orbital revolution have on the angles and duration of illumination across the globe. This is because the resulting cycles of change in sun angles and day lengths are the basis for climatic seasonality and many biological activities.

As the Earth revolves about the Sun, the position of the axis of rotation within the *circle of illumination* changes. At the points of Equinox: the circle of illumination passes through both poles and day length is equal at all latitudes; the subsolar point is at the Equator; and the solar noon Sun angle (measured from local horizons) is the complimentary angle of the latitude at all locations. At the points of Solstice: the rotational axis differs by 23.5° from the plane defined by the circle of illumination; day length varies from 0 to 24 hours over the Earth; the subsolar point is at one of the Tropics and solar noon Sun angle at all locations differs from the complimentary angle by 23.5°. In navigation, measuring solar noon angle allows for the determination of latitude. Table 1 below provides a summary of solar declination for the year.

While there are many similar formulas you can use, a simple expression to calculate solar geometry is: **Solar noon Sun angle = 90° - | latitude – current date declination |**

Note that declination values are conventionally given as ***positive*** values in the northern hemisphere and ***negative*** values in the southern hemisphere. Also, use of the straight bracket (|) in the second equation denotes that the absolute value of the value in brackets is to be subtracted from 90°. For any given day, there will be two points on the Earth's surface that will have the same solar noon sun angle.

As the angle of incidence between the Sun's rays and the atmosphere declines, each unit of incoming solar energy is dispersed over a larger area. This is a major reason for the lower solar intensity at higher latitudes.

Table 1. Solar Declination throughout the year (or, latitude of the subsolar point)

Date		Degrees	Date		Degrees
January	1	-23	June	30	+23
January	10	-22	July	10	+22.5
January	20	-20	July	20	+21
January	30	-17.5	July	30	+18.5
February	10	-15	August	10	+16
February	20	-11	August	20	+12.5
March	1	-8	August	30	+9
March	10	-4.5	September	10	+5
March	20	-0.5	September	20	+1.5
March	30	+3.5	September	30	-2.5
April	10	+7.5	October	10	-6.5
April	20	+11	October	20	-10
April	30	+14.5	October	30	-13.5
May	10	+17	November	10	-17
May	20	+20	November	20	-19.5
May	30	+22	November	30	-21.5
June	10	+23	December	10	-23
June	20	+23.5	December	20	-23.5

Radiation Budgets

Assuming there has been no change in the incoming (extra-terrestrial) solar radiation, K_{EX}, or in average cloud cover throughout Earth's recent history, the radiation balance for the Earth has varied drastically over time. Short and long-wave radiation balances interfacing between the earth's surface, its atmosphere and space for the present day climate (PDC) compared to a glacial climate (GC), such as existed on earth 20,000 years ago when roughly one-half of the earth's surface was dominated by glacial ice and sea ice, are vastly different. The differences observed between present-day climate and glacial climate is important for understanding the difference between present-day low latitude and present-day high latitude climates as the temperature of the air at high latitudes is much cooler than lower latitudes.

Lab Test 1 Preparation

Lab Test 1 – Solar Geometry and Radiation Budgets will test your understanding of the change in solar noon sun angle with latitude, and the difference in radiation budgets from present day climates to glacial climates or low-latitude vs. high-latitude climates.

Preparation: To prepare for Lab Test 1, review the Lab 1 podcast and complete the sample questions below, comparing your answers to the solutions posted on Avenue. Study the material, make sure you know all equations and understand all concepts such that you can apply them to more complex problems.

Materials required: You must bring a pencil, eraser, pen, and calculator to complete Lab Test 1

Solar Geometry *Sample* Questions

Show all of your calculations, including units.

1. Assuming it is solar noon, determine the following (show all of your calculations):
    a. your latitude, if the solar noon Sun angle measures **55°** at the **June solstice**

    $$\text{Solar Sun angle} = 90° - |L - \text{current date declination}|$$
    $$55° = 90 - |L - 23.5|$$
    $$|L - 23.5| = 35° \approx |L - 23.5| = \pm 35$$
    $$L = \pm 35 + 23.5, \quad L = 58.5° N, 11.5° S$$

    b. your latitude if the Sun angle measures **25°** at the **December solstice**

    $$25° = 90° - |L - (-23.5)|$$
    $$|L - (-23.5)| = 65° \approx L + 23.5 = \pm 65°$$
    $$L = \pm 65 - 23.5$$
    $$L = 88.5° N, -41.5° S$$

    c. the Sun angle at **30°S** on *March 10th*

    $$S = 90° - |(-30) - (-4.5)|$$
    $$S = 90° - |-25.5|$$
    $$S = 90° - 25.5$$
    $$S = 64.5°$$

    d. the Sun angle in **Hamilton (43°N)** on *September 30th*

    $$S = 90° - |43 - (-2.5)|$$
    $$S = 90° - |43 + 2.5|$$
    $$S = 90° - 45.5$$
    $$S = 44.5°$$

Radiation Budgets *Sample* Questions

Consult Table 2 which gives the solar radiation, long-wave radiation and surface heat fluxes for a present day climate (PDC) and glacial climate (GC) and complete the following:

1. Complete the attached flow chart (Figure 1) using the radiation data presented in Table 2. Differentiate between solar radiation, long-wave radiation, and the surface heat fluxes by highlighting each with a different colour and provide a legend.

2. In Table 3 enter the radiation data for the balance to space, at the earth's surface and within the atmosphere for the present day and for the glacial climate. The incoming and outgoing radiation must balance for each climate type.

Table 2: Radiation values for present day climate (PDC) and glacial climate (GC). The cloud cover is assumed to be constant at 5/10.

Solar Radiation		PDC	GC
K_{EX}	Extraterrestrial solar radiation	100	100
C_r	Cloud reflection to space	20	18
K_{f1}	Cloud reflection downward	8	9
Ar	Atmospheric reflection to space	6	5
K_{f2}	Atmospheric reflection downward	13	12
Sr	Earth surface reflection to space	4	21
A_a	Atmospheric Absorption	25	19
K_d	Diffused	24	16

Long-wave Radiation			
L_a	Longwave radiation from surface absorbed in the atmosphere	96	68
L_s	Longwave from surface to space through atmospheric window	17	7
L_{as}	Longwave from atmosphere to space	53	49
L_{as}	Longwave from atmosphere to surface	97	65

Surface Heat Fluxes			
Q_E	Latent heat of evapotranspiration	23	16
Q_H	Sensible heat flux from surface to atmosphere	6	11

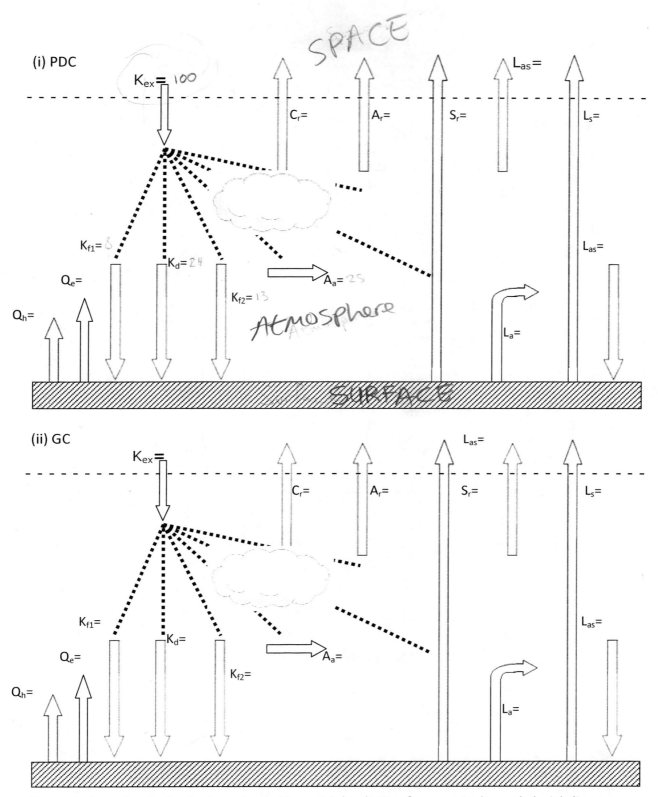

Figure 1: Incoming and outgoing solar and terrestrial radiation for present day and glacial climates.

29

Table 3: Solar Radiation table for balancing

Balance to Space					Surface Balance					Atmospheric Balance				
S	PDC In	PDC Out	GC In	GC Out	S	PDC In	PDC Out	GC In	GC Out	S	PDC In	PDC Out	GC In	GC Out
Kex		100		100	Qu		6		11	Qu	6		11	
Cr	20		18		Qe		23		16	Qe	23		16	
Ar	6		5		Ia	8	96	9	68	Ia	96		68	
Sr	4		21		$K_{\downarrow}f_{\downarrow}$	24		6		Aa	25		19	
Las	53		49		$P_{\uparrow}f_{\uparrow}$	13		12						
S	17		7		Las	97		59		Los↑		53		49
					L↑		17		7	Las↓		97		65
Total	100	100	100			142	142	107	102		150	150	144	144

Lab Test 2 – Environmental Lapse Rates
Adiabatic Warming/Cooling of Rising Air

Preparation: Watch the Lab 2 Tutorial on A2L, complete the sample questions provided, and study/understand all equations and concepts

Worth: 7.5% of your final mark

Introduction: Week of February 2nd

Lab Test 2:   In Lab the week of February 9th

Introduction

DALR and SALR

The word "adiabatic" comes from the Greek word adiabatos, meaning "impassable". What is impassable? A certain volume of air is imagined to have impenetrable boundaries on all sides. When the rise and descent of the air is very rapid, as it would be in the powerful downdraft of a Chinook descending the lee side of the Rockies, the dry adiabatic lapse rate holds true for all practical purposes.

Environmental Lapse Rate

The environmental lapse rate is of great importance in understanding how weather works in the troposphere. Generally, the air gets colder as you go higher. Why should that be so? Think of being close to a roaring bonfire; you feel warm, of course. Slowly, you back away from the fire; the warmth diminishes with distance. In this analogy, the earth's surface is the bonfire, heated by absorption of the sun's radiant energy. As you ascend, you move away from the radiating heat source and the air becomes cooler (Strahler and Strahler, 1989).

Adiabatic Lapse Rate: rate at which an air parcel cools as it rises in altitude through convection. No heat transfer occurs into or out of the air parcel as it cools down.

Dry adiabatic lapse rate (DALR): rate of temperature decrease with altitude for a parcel of dry or unsaturated air as it rises

Saturated adiabatic lapse rate (SALR): rate of temperature decrease with altitude for a parcel of air saturated with water vapour as it rises. The SALR varies with temperature

Lab Test 2 Preparation

Lab Test 2 – Environmental Lapse Rates will test your understanding of the changes in temperature of dry and saturated air masses as they move to higher or lower altitudes.

Preparation: To prepare for Lab Test 2, review the Lab 2 podcast and complete the sample questions below, comparing your answers to the solutions posted on Avenue. Study the material, make sure you know all equations and understand all concepts such that you can apply them to more complex problems.

Materials required: You must bring a pencil, eraser, pen, and calculator to complete Lab Test 2

Environmental Lapse Rates Sample Questions

Show all of your calculations, including units.

A mass of rising air will cool along the dry adiabatic lapse rate of (10°C/km) until it reaches the condensation level at which point it will continue to rise along the saturated adiabatic lapse rate (6°C/km). A mass of air has a dew point temperature of **4°C** and a temperature at the Earth's surface of **16°C**.

(handwritten: DALR = 10°C/km)

(handwritten left margin diagram: Temp at 2300M, SALR =6°C, DALR =10°C/km, 4°C DP, E = 16°C)

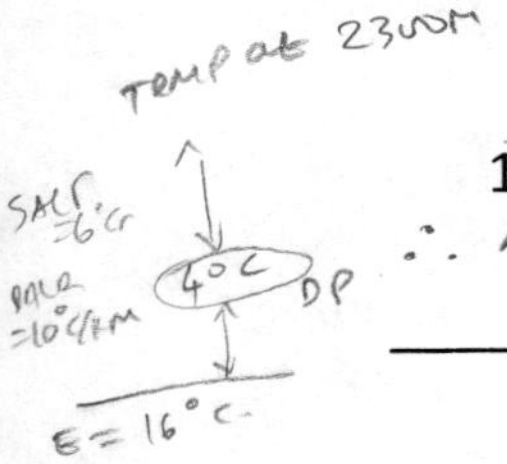

1. At what altitude will the condensation level be reached? Show your calculations.

(handwritten: ∴ ΔTemp°C = 16°C − 4°C = 12°C   ∴ Altitude = 12°C ÷ 10°C = 1.2 km)

2. What will the temperature of the air mass be at **2300 m** above the Earth's surface? Show your calculations.

(handwritten: Height above due point = 2.3km − 1.2km = 1.1km)

(handwritten: Temp°C change = 1.1km × -6°c = -6.6°C)

(handwritten: Temp°C at 2300 = 4°c + -6.6°C = -2.6°C)

In Ludington, Michigan (43°N 86°W) on a mild afternoon in March, the surface air temperature is **13°C**. A vertical sounding of the atmosphere by balloon reveals a nearly constant temperature lapse rate of 10°C per kilometre. At the tropopause a temperature of **-38°C** is recorded. The elevation of Ludington, Michigan is **593 m** above sea level.

3. What is the correct equation to calculate the tropopause in metres above sea level? Circle the correct answer.
   a. Δ T/ELR + Michigan alt.   *or Δ height × ELR + M Alt*
   b. ELR/ Δ T + Michigan alt.
   c. Δ T/ELR - Michigan alt.
   d. Δ T x ELR + Michigan alt.

   (a is circled)

4. What is the level of the tropopause in meters above sea level? Show your calculations

   Δ temp °C = 13°C − −38°C = 51°C

   level = 51°C ÷ 10°C = 5.1 km = 5100 m

   ∴ 5100 + 593 m = 5693 m

office hours GSb

Lab Test 3 – Water Balance

Preparation: Watch the Lab 3 Tutorial on A2L, complete the sample questions provided, and study/understand all equations and concepts

Worth: 7.5% of your final mark

Introduction: Week of March 2nd

Lab Test 3:   In Lab the week of March 9th

Introduction

The water balance method is a tool used to calculate the net accumulation of inputs and outputs of water for specific locations (agricultural field, drainage basin or country). In order to determine water balance for a year, input (precipitation), output (evapotranspiration) and storage changes of water are calculated. These calculations are recorded in tabular form and presented in graphical form. The water balance approach was introduced by Thornthwaite in 1948 and is used to assess water resources for use in irrigation and other water related issues. Table 2 gives water balance calculations for Hamilton and Figure 2 shows Hamilton's water balance in graphical form. The calculations include the following parts:

Potential Evapotranspiration (PE): is the amount of evapotranspiration (evaporation + transpiration) which would occur if the water supply was unlimited and conditions were optimal. PE is given as a depth of water in mm and represents the demand that the atmosphere makes on the available water supply. This demand is a function of solar or radiant energy supply (net radiation, Q*) at the surface, atmospheric temperature (T_a) and atmospheric vapour pressure deficit (VPD). Since temperature is the most common worldwide climate measurement, it allows potential evapotranspiration to be calculated for thousands of places around the globe.

Table 1 shows that for Hamilton **PE = 0 in the winter months when T_a< 0°C** and that PE reaches a maximum in the months of June, July and August when T_a is largest. **Quantity given.**

Precipitation (P): Commonly measured quantity and is normally used based on a 30 year average which is available for most land areas of the world. Table 2 indicates that precipitation in Hamilton is very even throughout the year so that when compared to PE: P>PE in winter and P<PE in summer. **Quantity given.**

P-PE: Quantity calculation- _P-PE_

35

Accumulated Potential Water Loss (ACC WL): The water deficit in summer is accumulated on a month by month basis. **Quantity calculation-** *Running sum of negative P-PE values.*

Soil Water Storage (ST): Soil moisture storage describes the quantity of water retained within the soil at any particular time. It is recognized that the soil water storage capacity can vary widely depending on soil type and the rooting depths of vegetation. For purposes of comparing different stations, a common average value of 300 mm storage capacity is used. For Hamilton the storage capacity is reached in January and maintained through May. **Quantity calculation-** *Using ACC WL find values on the attached graph (fig 1). Then take the last ST value and add it to P-PE for each subsequent month creating another running sum. Do this until 300 is reached and then maintain.*

Soil Water Storage Change (ΔST): The quantity of water that is added or removed from the water being stored is known as soil water storage change. When P<PE and an ACC WL develops, water is removed from the soil reservoir; however, as the ACC WL grows larger it becomes increasingly difficult to remove water from the soil. This is shown in Figure 1 which plots ST against ACC WL. The curve is non-linear so that as ACC WL grows large, the decrease in ST becomes less rapid. Such a feature is realistic because as soils dry, they exert suction forces which retain the remaining soil water more strongly. By using the ACC WL on the horizontal axis and reading the ST on the vertical axis, the ST value can be entered in Row 5. ΔST in Row 6 then becomes:

$$\Delta ST_M = ST_{M-1} - ST_M$$

where M is the month. In the case of Hamilton during the dry summer period, M is initially June and M-1 is May. For June $\Delta ST_M = ST_{M-1} - ST_M$

$$= ST_{MAY} - ST_{JUNE}$$
$$= 300 - 254$$
$$= 46$$

When P>PE, the extra water goes into recharging the soil water until the Field Capacity of 300 mm is reached. For Hamilton this occurs during October, November, December and early January. Sometimes there is never enough precipitation to recharge the soil to field capacity, so that an ACC WL always exists. Examples of this are encountered in this Lab. **Quantity calculation-** *When ACC WL exists ΔST= ST for the previous month minus ST for the present month.*

Actual Evapotranspiration (AE): Quantity calculation- *If $P \geq PE$ AE = PE*
If $P < PE$ AE = P +Δ ST

Water Deficit (D): It is evident in the case of Hamilton that there is a small water deficit in the months of June through September. **Quantity calculation-** *If P<PE then D = PE – AE.*

Water Surplus (S): Water surplus occurs when the soil water is at field capacity, meaning that the soil is at maximum water retention. This water becomes runoff to feed the streams. If the surplus occurs as winter snow, it is often held in storage until the spring, before runoff occurs.

For Hamilton, a water surplus starts in January. For the month of January, 6 mm of the extra P is used to raise ST to field capacity at 300 mm and the rest is realized as surplus. For the months February through May, S = P-PE. **Quantity calculation-** *When P>PE: For first month that P>PE subtract the last month, before ST was 300, from 300 and then subtract this number from the actual value of P-PE for that month. For all other months S=P-PE.*

REFERENCE:
Thornthwaite, C.W. 1948. An approach toward a rational classification of climate. Geographical Review XXXVIII, 55-

Table 1: Potential evaporation and water deficit/surplus magnitudes.

	RANGE				
	Very Low	**Low**	**Moderate**	**Large**	**Very Large**
Temperature Range = $PE_{Max} - PE_{Min}$ (ie. Max *minus* Min)	0-24	25-74	75-124	125-174	175 +
Water deficit/surplus (Total value)	0-24	25-74	75-249	250-749	750 +

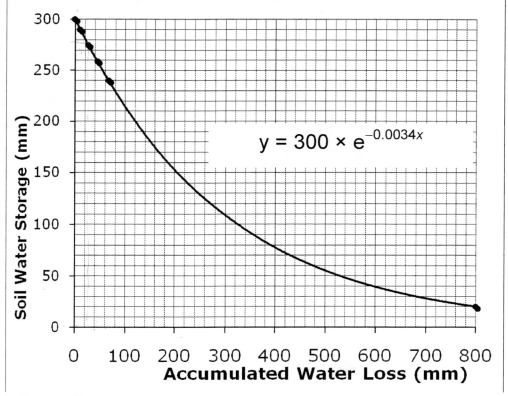

Figure 1: Soil Water Storage

Table 2: Hamilton water balance

	J	F	M	A	M	J	J	A	S	O	N	D	TOTAL
PE	0	0	0	30	72	111	135	122	84	48	15	0	617
P	63	57	66	67	73	63	81	67	61	62	67	64	791
P-PE	63	57	66	37	1	-48	-54	-55	-23	14	52	64	174
ACC WL						48	102	157	180				
ST	300	300	300	300	300	254	212	178	164	178	230	294	
ΔST						46	42	34	14				
AE	0	0	0	30	72	109	123	101	75	48	15	0	573
D						2	12	21	9				44
S	57	57	66	37	1								218

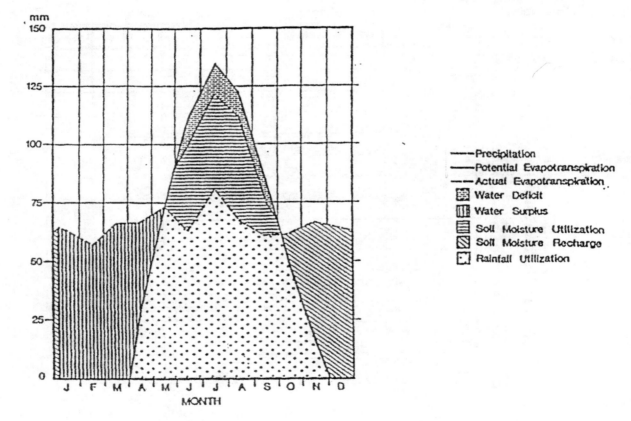

Figure 2: Diagram showing the components of the Hamilton water balance.

Lab Test 3 Preparation

Lab Test 3 – Water Balance will test your ability to calculate water balance tables and to interpret the results.

Preparation: To prepare for Lab Test 3, review the Lab 3 podcast and complete the sample questions below, comparing your answers to the solutions posted on Avenue. Study the material, make sure you know **all equations** and understand all concepts such that you can apply them to more complex problems.

Materials Required: You must bring a pencil, eraser, pen, calculator, and coloured pencils to complete Lab Test 3

Water Balance *Sample* Questions

Complete the following questions for Stations A and B using the data provided.

1. Complete the water tables. **Show** that your water tables balance using the calculation: P-S+D=PE

2. Identify the following areas on each of the graphs: Water Deficit, Water Recharge, Water Surplus, Soil Moisture Utilization and Rainfall Utilization.

3. Interpret the data by determining the following:
   a. Hemisphere
   b. Length of the growing season
   c. Temperature patterns
   d. Temperature range *(use Table 1)*
   e. Precipitation patterns/range
   f. Timing and magnitude of water surplus *(use Table 1)*
   g. Timing and magnitude of water deficit *(use Table 1)*
   h. Continentality of station

STATION A:

	J	F	M	A	M	J	J	A	S	O	N	D	TOTAL
PE	0	3	20	53	97	127	147	132	89	48	18	5	739
P	48	46	46	53	74	97	61	56	51	56	61	56	705
P-PE	48	43	26	0	-23	-30	-86	-76	-38	8	43	51	-34
ACC WL					23	53	139	215	253				
ST	277	300	300	300	277	251	187	144	127	135	178	229	
ΔST					-23	26	64	43	17				
AE	0	3	20	53	97	123	125	99	68	48	18	5	659
D					0	4	22	33	21				80
S	48	20	26	0						8	43	51	46

f = 300 instead of 320.

Balance:

Water Balance For Station A

Hemisphere	Length of Growing Season	Temperature Patterns	Temperature Range	Precipitation Patterns	Timing & Magnitude of Water Surplus	Timing & Magnitude of Water Deficit	Continentality
Northern	11 month	warm winter	large	year round with summer max	low winter	moderate summer	concurrent

40

STATION B:

	J	F	M	A	M	J	J	A	S	O	N	D	TOTAL
PE	94	86	98	95	92	84	87	93	95	105	99	98	1126
P	292	347	342	225	111	16	1	3	14	25	28	139	1543
P-PE	198	261	244	130	19	-68	-86	-90	-81	-80	-71	41	417
ACC WL						68	154	244	325	405	476		
ST	298	300	300	300	300	238	178	131	99	76	59	100	
ΔST						62	60	47	32	23	17		
AE	94	86	98	95	92	78	61	50	46	48	45	98	891
D						6	26	43	49	57	54		235
S		259	244	130	19								652

F=300 instead of 359

261

Balance:

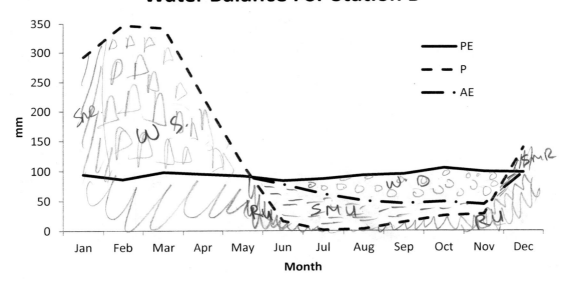

Hemisphere	Length of Growing Season	Temperature Patterns	Temperature Range	Precipitation Patterns	Timing & Magnitude of Water Surplus	Timing & Magnitude of Water Deficit	Continentality
southern	12 months	Hot summer, warm winter	very low	year round summer max.	large summer	Moderate winter/spring	maritime

41

Lab Test 4 – Weather Maps

Preparation: Watch the Lab 4 Tutorial on A2L, complete the sample questions provided, and study/understand all equations and concepts

Worth: 7.5% of your final mark

Introduction: Week of March 16th

Lab Test 4: In Lab the week of March 23rd

Weather Maps

Analyzing maps with the current weather conditions is an essential part of the entire forecast process. Basically, if we do not know what is currently occurring, it is near impossible to predict what will happen in the future.

Computers have been able to analyze maps for over 20 years. However, computers cannot interpret what they analyze. There is no substitute for the hand analysis. Analyzing maps by hand causes the forecaster to study every detail in the weather and enables him/her to discern the continuity or "flow" of the weather.

Great forecasts, the ones that save lives and property, begin with the careful analysis of the current conditions. Conversely, based upon post-analysis, "bad" (or busted) forecasts, the ones most remembered by the public, could have been improved if one did a careful analysis in the beginning.

Highlighting the spatial patterns of specific variables such as temperature, pressure, and weather fronts is a first step in weather analysis. Isolines are often used for this purpose. Each type of isoline is named to reflect the variable being mapped: isotherms are the lines of constant temperature and isobars are lines of constant barometric pressure; **These lines are smooth and do not cross each other.**

Lab Test 4 Preparation

Lab Test 4 – Weather Maps will test your understanding and analysis of isotherms, pressure patterns, and weather patterns along fronts.

Preparation: To prepare for Lab Test 4, review the Lab 4 podcast and complete the sample questions below, comparing your answers to the solutions posted on Avenue. Study the material, make sure you understand all concepts such that you can apply them to more complex problems.

Materials Required: You must bring a pencil, eraser, pen, and **coloured pencils** to complete Lab Test 4

Weather Maps Sample Questions

MAPPING ISOTHERMS

Attached is a figure of a Simple Station Model as well as a weather map of part of Canada. The Simple Station Model indicates how weather at each weather recording station is presented on the weather map. One piece of information recorded on a weather map is the current temperature at each recording station. Highlight the temperature at each station on the map. Using a blue coloured pencil, lightly draw and label lines connecting equal values of temperatures (i.e. isotherms), every 5°C (e.g. -5, 0, 5, 10°C etc.). Make sure to label each isotherm.

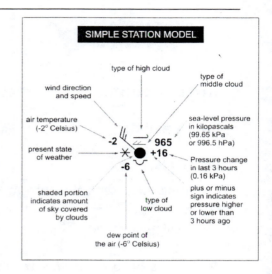

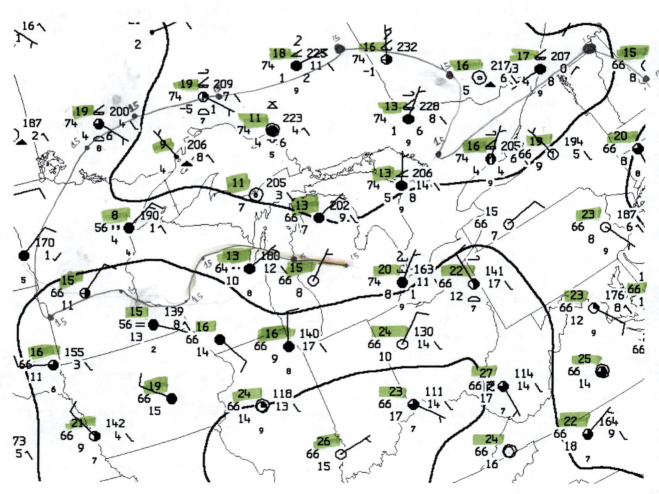

ATMOSPHERIC PRESSURE

Below is a weather map from the Northern Hemisphere. The lines on the weather map are isobars, which represent lines of constant barometric pressure. Pressures are also given at each High and Low. Answer the following questions using information from the map.

What is the highest pressure found on this map? _____1016_____

What is the lowest pressure found on this map? _____980_____

Which regions would you *expect* to see precipitation- around highs or lows? On the map, shade these regions in green. L

Which regions would you *expect* to see fair weather- around highs or lows? On the map, shade these regions in yellow. H

Using arrows, draw the wind direction around the low and high pressure areas (ie. clockwise or counterclockwise arrows)

Identify 1 region with a strong pressure gradient by writing 'strong' on the map in the corresponding location.

Identify 1 region with a weak pressure gradient by writing 'weak' on the map in the corresponding location.

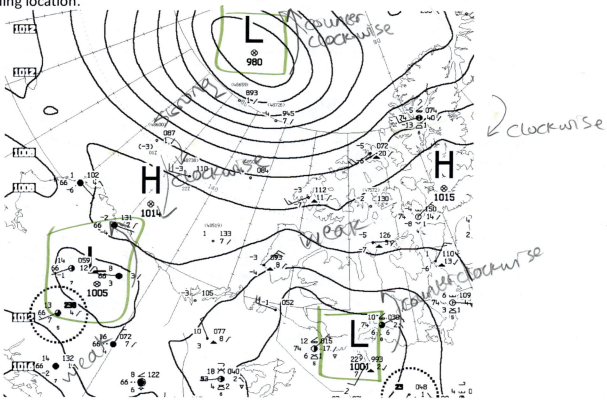

FRONTS

Below is a weather map with stations labelled A-F. Answer the following questions using information from the map.

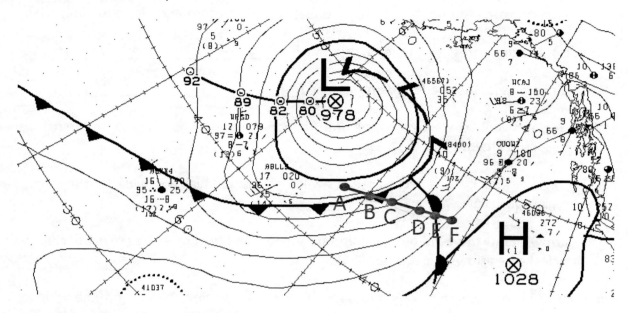

What types of fronts are found on this surface map? _cold & warm_

Along which type of front would you expect to see heavy precipitation/thunderstorms?
warm

Along which type of front would you expect to see light precipitation that may last for several days? _cold_

Overrunning occurs along which type of front? _cold_

You are outside gardening and notice cirrus clouds in the sky. What weather might you expect to follow?
Hailstorms or Ice supercooled water droplets

In the space below, draw a vertical cross section along the line from stations A-F. Label the air masses and indicate the positions of stations A-F. Make sure your diagram indicates appropriate differences between the slopes of the fronts. No depiction of clouds or weather is required.

46

Part III: References and Acknowledgements

References

Briggs, David, Peter Smithson and Timothy Ball. 1989. Fundamentals of Physical Geography. 2nd ed. Toronto: Copp Clark Pitman Ltd.

Canada Department of Energy, Mines and Resources, Surveys, Mapping and Remote Sensing Sector. 1986. National Atlas of Canada. 5th ed.

Canada National Committee for the International Hydrological Decade. 1978. Hydrological Atlas of Canada. Ottawa: Fisheries and Environment Canada.

Henderson-Sellers, A. and P.J. Robinson. 1986. Contemporary Climatology. New York: Wiley.

Hengeveld, Henry. 1995. Understanding Atmospheric Change: A Survey of the Background Science and Implications of Climate Change and Ozone Depletion. State of the Environment Report No. 95-2. Ottawa: Environment Canada.

Standford, Quentin H. 1992. Canadian Oxford World Atlas. Toronto: Oxford University Press.

Tarbuck, Edward J., Frederick K. Lutgens and Kenneth G. Pinzke. 1997. Applications and Investigations in Earth Science. 2nd ed. Toronto: Prentice Hall.

Acknowledgements

This custom courseware is based on previous editions of the custom courseware for Environmental Science 1A03 by Susan Vajoczki.